WE ARE MUSLIMS

Aqidah, Fiqh, and *Aklaq*

A Textbook

FOR

GRADE TWO

Dr. Abidullah Ghazi
Dr. Tasneema Ghazi

IQRA' International Educational Foundation

Part of a Comprehensive and Systematic Program of Islamic Studies

A Textbook for the program of *Aqidah, Fiqh,* and *Aklaq*

**We are Muslims:
Grade:2**

Chief Program Editors
Dr. Abidullah Ghazi
(Ph.D., Study of Religion
Harvard University)

Dr. Tasneema Ghazi
(Ph.D., Curriculum-Reading
University of Minnesota)

Editing
Fadel I. Abdallah
Huseyin Abiva
Rahayu Mohamad

Illustrations
Brad Cornelius

Design
Robinson Design
Aliuddin Khaja

First Edition March, 2006
Second Printing August, 2008
Third Printing March, 2010
Printed in India

Library of Congress Catalog Card Number:94-65596
ISBN # 1-56316-074-9

IQRA'S NOTE

As-Salamu 'Alaikum!

This textbook, *WE ARE MUSLIMS* Book 2, is a part of IQRA's systematic and comprehensive program of Islamic education. This program has been designed to produce a quality and integrated religious educational system for the Islamic schools in North America and other parts of the English-speaking world. It is hoped that this curriculum will facilitate the teaching of the Islamic knowledge within a cross-curricular setting. It has also been designed to make use of modern technology and critical thinking skills in the teaching and learning processes.

WE ARE MUSLIMS Book 2 introduces the basic tenets of the Islamic faith, Islamic ways of *Ibadah* and *Akhlaq* to 7 - 8 year olds at their level of understanding. The authors have made special efforts to help pupils learn and practice Islamic manners, especially within the boundaries of familial relationships.

This textbook has been written in the simple and lucid language of the Second Grade reading level. The readability level of the text has been carefully evaluated to suit the beginning readers. It is hoped that the pupils will be able to comprehend the concepts introduced in each lesson and adopt the teachings in their everyday life.

It is recommended that teachers use the accompanying workbook along with the textbook during class time. The workbook has been prepared to provide pupils with important exercises in comprehension as well as to aid in the development of critical thinking skills.

We invite you to join hands in our efforts and send us your comments and suggestions. It is only through joint endeavours that we can build a viable and professional program of education for our children.

Chief Editors
IQRA' International Educational Foundation
Chicago, IL. USA

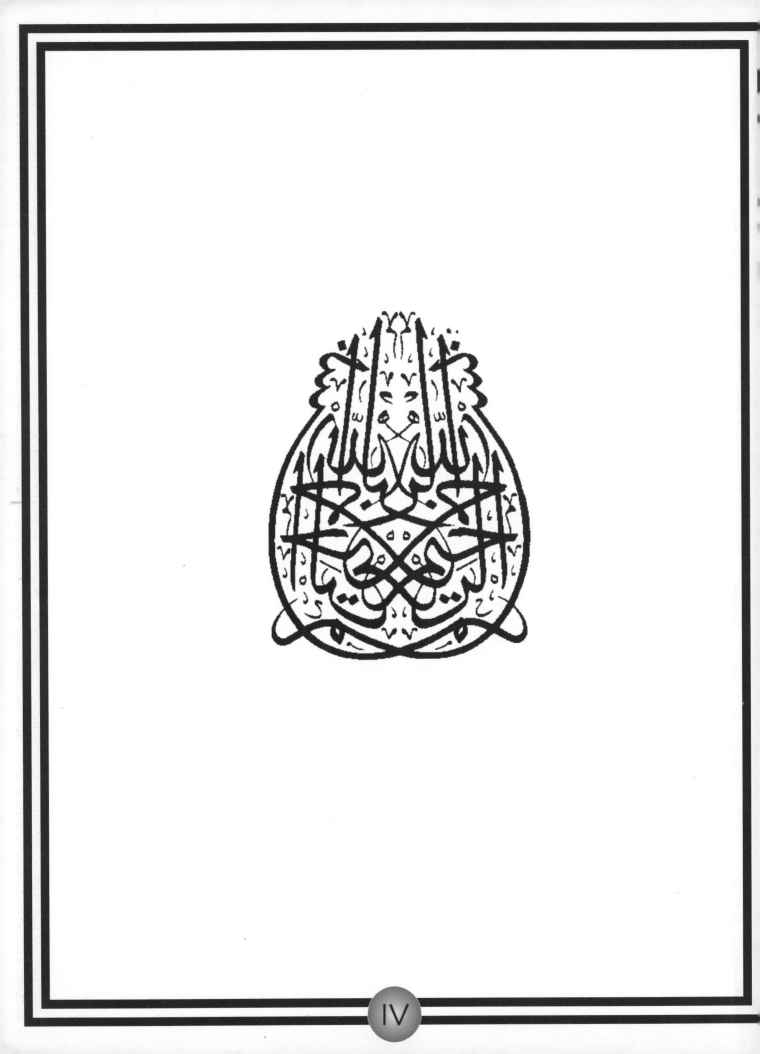

About the Book
The following write up presents highlights on the features of the textbook.

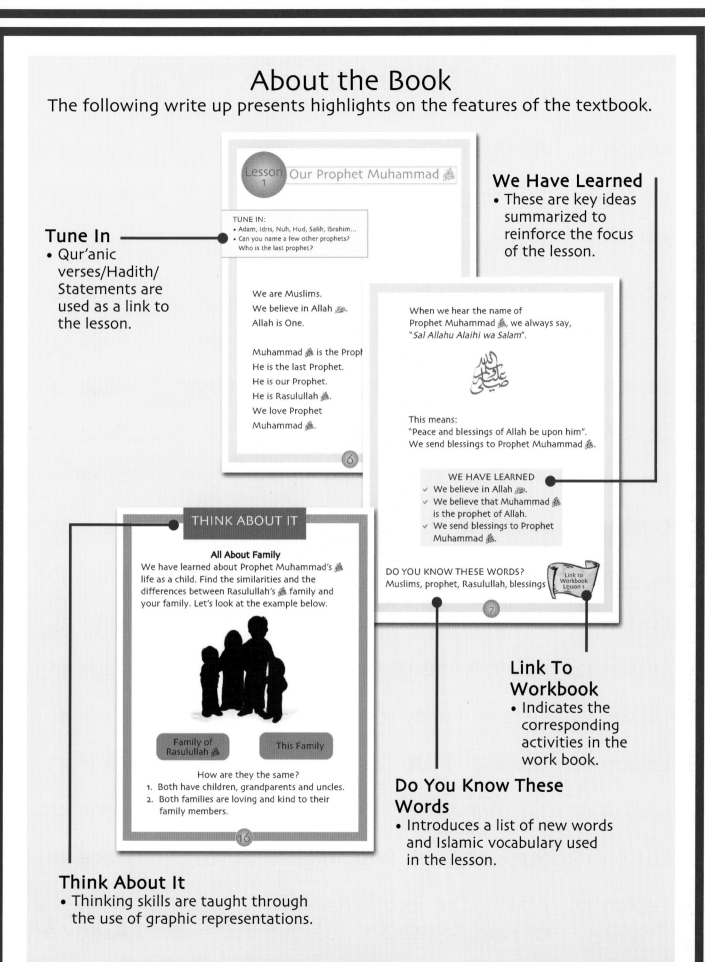

Lesson 1 Our Prophet Muhammad ﷺ

TUNE IN:
- Adam, Idris, Nuh, Hud, Salih, Ibrahim...
- Can you name a few other prophets? Who is the last prophet?

We are Muslims.
We believe in Allah ﷻ.
Allah is One.

Muhammad ﷺ is the Proph
He is the last Prophet.
He is our Prophet.
He is Rasulullah ﷺ.
We love Prophet
Muhammad ﷺ.

6

Tune In
- Qur'anic verses/Hadith/ Statements are used as a link to the lesson.

When we hear the name of Prophet Muhammad ﷺ, we always say, "*Sal Allahu Alaihi wa Salam*".

This means:
"Peace and blessings of Allah be upon him".
We send blessings to Prophet Muhammad ﷺ.

WE HAVE LEARNED
- ✓ We believe in Allah ﷻ.
- ✓ We believe that Muhammad ﷺ is the prophet of Allah.
- ✓ We send blessings to Prophet Muhammad ﷺ.

DO YOU KNOW THESE WORDS?
Muslims, prophet, Rasulullah, blessings

Link to Workbook Lesson 1

7

We Have Learned
- These are key ideas summarized to reinforce the focus of the lesson.

THINK ABOUT IT

All About Family
We have learned about Prophet Muhammad's ﷺ life as a child. Find the similarities and the differences between Rasulullah's ﷺ family and your family. Let's look at the example below.

Family of Rasulullah ﷺ   This Family

How are they the same?
1. Both have children, grandparents and uncles.
2. Both families are loving and kind to their family members.

16

Link To Workbook
- Indicates the corresponding activities in the work book.

Do You Know These Words
- Introduces a list of new words and Islamic vocabulary used in the lesson.

Think About It
- Thinking skills are taught through the use of graphic representations.

V

Table of Contents

Table of Contents

TUNE IN:

- Do you know how to say "May the Peace (of Allah) be on you" in Arabic? Let us find out!

Aliya and Jibraan are cousins and neighbors. They are Muslim children.

When they meet with each other, they always say, *"As-Salamu 'Alaikum"*. This means "May the Peace (of Allah) be on you".

Allah ﷻ wants us to live in peace with everyone. We say *Salam* to everyone. We wish *"As-Salamu 'Alaikum"* to everyone we meet. We wish peace for everyone.

When someone says *"As-Salamu 'Alaikum"* to us first, we should always reply and say *"Wa 'Alaikum us-Salam"*. It means "May the Peace (of Allah) be on you too".

When we say "*Wa 'Alaikum us-Salam*", we are asking Allah ﷻ to send peace to that person.

Our Prophet Muhammad ﷺ told us to try to be the first one to say "*As-Salamu 'Alaikum*" when we meet someone. He used to say "*As-Salamu 'Alaikum*" first when he met someone.

When we wish to speak to someone, we do so after greeting them. Prophet Muhammad told us:

"Greet each other with *Salam*."(Al-Tirmidhi)

Let us also remember to return the *Salam* by saying "*Wa 'Alaikum us-Salam*" when someone says *Salam* to us.

When Muslims meet other Muslims, they not only greet each other with nice words, but they also ask for Allah's blessings and mercy upon them.

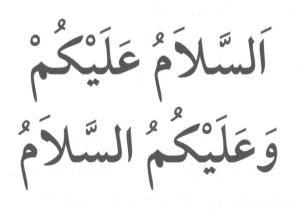

May Allah ﷻ help us to live in peace with each other and take care of one another.

DO YOU KNOW THESE WORDS?
- Lord
- greeting
- Peace
- mercy
- cousin

Link to Workbook Lesson 1

TUNE IN:

- Every group of people has a special way of greeting. Let us find out how we can greet our non-Muslim friends and neighbors.

We greet others to show our respect and our good wishes for them. Every group of people has a special way of greeting.

The Chinese people say "Nee How."
The Spanish people greet each other with "¡Hola!"
In our country, people say "Hello."
Can you find out the meaning of these greetings?

A Muslim greets another Muslim by saying *"As-Salamu 'Alaikum"*. This means "May the Peace (of Allah) be on you."

Today we use greetings that are common to all. When we meet our friends and neighbors who are not Muslim we can say "Hello", "Good Morning" or "Good Evening".

When we meet our neighbors who are not Muslims, we must always be polite to them. We must greet them with the best greetings that they use and understand. We must also respond politely to their greetings.

WE HAVE LEARNED

- The greeting of Islam is *"As-Salamu 'Alaikum"*.
- We can say "Hello", "Good Morning" or "Good Evening" to greet our friends and neighbours who are not Muslims.
- We must greet everyone with the best greetings that they understand.

DO YOU KNOW THESE WORDS?
- greetings
- Hispanic
- Chinese
- Polite

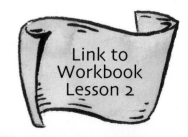
Link to Workbook Lesson 2

TUNE IN:
- Do you know what the responsibilities of a Muslim are? A Muslim's responsibilities to Allah are to believe in Allah, His *Mala'ikah*, His Books, His Prophets, the *Akhirah, al-Qadr*, Allah's power over everyone and life after death.

Aliya and Jibraan are Muslim children. They believe that there is no god but Allah ﷾ and Muhammad ﷺ is His Messenger.

All Muslims have the same beliefs as Aliya and Jibraan. They all must say this belief with their tongues and accept it in their hearts.

What is *Iman Muffassal*?

Iman Mufassal means "Complete Faith." We can learn the *Iman Mufassal* in Arabic and understand its meaning. Let us read:

$$\text{اَمَنْتُ بِاللّٰهِ وَمَلَائِكَتِهِ وَكُتُبِهِ وَرُسُلِهِ ، وَالْيَوْمِ الْأَخِرِ ،}$$

$$\text{وَالْقَدَرِ خَيْرِهِ وَشَرِّهِ مِنَ اللّٰهِ تَعَالَى ،}$$

$$\text{وَالْبَعْثِ بَعْدَ الْمَوْتِ}$$

"I believe in Allah, and in His Angels, and in His Books, and in His Prophets, and in the Last Day, and in *al-Qadr* (the Power) to do good or bad is from Allah ﷻ and in life after death."

Aliya's mother told the children that all Muslims believe in One God, who is our Lord and Creator. He sent many prophets and messengers to all the people of the world. These prophets taught people how to live in peace and how to pray to Allah ﷻ.

Allah ﷻ sent many books to lead humankind to the path of Islam. Allah ﷻ created angels from *Nur*, Light. He created angels to serve and worship Him. He chose Angel Jibril ﷺ to bring His books to some of the prophets.

One day all of us will die. There is a life after death that will last forever. Allah ﷻ will bring us back to life again on the Day of Judgment.

Allah ﷻ is All-Powerful. He has power over everything. Whatever good or bad happens in this world is by His permission.

Believing in all these things makes one a Muslim.

WE HAVE LEARNED

- All Muslims have common beliefs.
- We must memorize *Iman Mufassal* and learn its meaning.
- A Muslim must believe in *Iman Mufassal*.

DO YOU KNOW THESE WORDS?
- *Iman Mufassal*
- Complete Faith
- forever
- permission
- Judgment

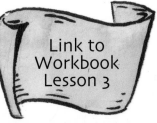

Link to Workbook Lesson 3

TUNE IN:

- Allah سبحانه وتعالى is our Creator. We have duties to Allah. We have to obey Allah's teachings. We have to remember Allah سبحانه وتعالى and always ask for help from Him.

Allah سبحانه وتعالى is our only God. He has created everyone. We believe there is no god but Allah سبحانه وتعالى. He is the only Creator.

There is no one like Allah سبحانه وتعالى. There is no one who shares His Power. Muslims pray only to Allah سبحانه وتعالى. We do not worship other gods besides Allah سبحانه وتعالى.

Allah سبحانه وتعالى has told us in the Qur'an to obey His teachings and follow His Book and His Prophet. It is our duty to obey His teachings.

It is our duty to remember Allah سبحانه وتعالى in our hearts and to remember Him in everything we do at all time. Our Prophet Muhammad ﷺ has taught us to say special words and praises to Allah ﷻ for the many beautiful things He has given us. We say "Al-Hamdulillah" to thank Him.

$$\text{اَلْحَمْدُ لِلَّه}$$

When we see something beautiful we praise Him with "Subhanallah".

Allah ﷻ is the only Provider. He is *Ar-Razzaq*. It is our duty to ask Allah's help when we start something and thank Him when we finish our work.

We ask Allah ﷻ to help us become good Muslims. We ask Him to help us to do only what makes Him happy.

These are our duties to Allah ﷻ. We have to obey Allah and thank Him for His help.

Remember Allah ﷻ at all times and Allah ﷻ will remember you

WE HAVE LEARNED

- Muslims must follow Allah's commands and teachings.
- We should always remember Allah ﷻ and pray only to Him.
- Allah ﷻ is the only Provider and we should always ask from Him.

DO YOU KNOW THESE WORDS?

- Provider
- *Ar-Razzaq*
- duty

- guide
- praise

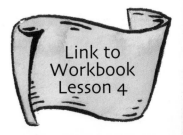

Link to Workbook Lesson 4

Lesson 5

We Obey Prophet Muhammad ﷺ

TUNE IN:

- Prophet Muhammad ﷺ is the Seal of the Prophets. What does it mean? Let us find out!

Prophet Muhammad ﷺ was a Prophet of Allah. He was the last Prophet. He was the last Messenger of Allah ﷻ.

He is called *Khatim Al-Anbiya*. It means the "Seal of the Prophets". He was the last and final Prophet of Allah. Allah ﷻ will not send any other prophet after him.

خَاتَمُ الأَنْبِيَاء

Allah ﷻ sent His last and final Message to Prophet Muhammad ﷺ. He sent the Qur'an to Prophet Muhammad ﷺ.

He has shown us how to live as good people in this world and obey Allah ﷻ.

What Do Muslims Follow?

Muslims follow the Qur'an. The Qur'an is the word of Allah ﷻ. We should follow the teachings of Prophet Muhammad ﷺ. We should try to do what he used to do.

When we follow Prophet Muhammad ﷺ, we are following his *Sunnah*. This will keep us on the right path.

Prophet Muhammad's words and his sayings are called the *Hadith*. We should read the *Hadith* of Prophet Muhammad and follow them.

Allah ﷻ is happy with us when we follow the *Sunnah* and the *Hadith*. When we follow the Sunnah and the *Hadith* of our Prophet Muhammad ﷺ, we are following Allah ﷻ.

How can we show our love towards Prophet Muhammad ﷺ?

We must always follow his *Sunnah* & *Hadith*.

WE HAVE LEARNED

- Prophet Muhammad ﷺ was the *Khatim Al-Anbiya*. This means the "Seal of the Prophets".
- *Qur'an* is the Book of Allah ﷻ.
- The sayings of Prophet Muhammad ﷺ are called *Hadith*.
- The actions of Prophet Muhammad ﷺ are called *Sunnah*

DO YOU KNOW THESE WORDS?
- *Khatim Al-Anbiya*
- *Sunnah*
- Seal of the Prophets
- *Hadith*

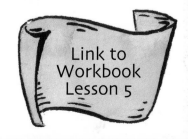

Link to Workbook Lesson 5

Lesson 6

Isma'il: A Responsible Muslim Boy

TUNE IN:

• Allah ﷻ wants us to take responsibility for everything we do and say.

This is Isma'il.

He lives in Chicago with his family. He is seven years old. He loves his family. He loves his city.

He likes to do his work on time. He gets up in the morning and goes to the bathroom. He brushes his teeth and makes *Wudu*.

He prays *Fajr* prayer. He makes *Zikr* and *Du'a*. He cleans his room and makes his bed. Then he takes a bath and puts on his clothes.

Isma'il always helps his mother to set the table for breakfast. He never forgets to greet his family members with *"As-Salamu 'Alaikum"* when they meet at the breakfast table. Everyone returns his greetings with *"Wa 'Alaikum us-Salam"*.

He helps his parents clean the table after breakfast. Isma'il thanks his mother for making a delicious breakfast. He thanks Allah for the food and says *"Al-Hamdulillah"*.

Then he gets ready and leaves for school with his sister, Isra.

Ismail's teacher is Mr. Ahmad. Isma'il walks into the classroom after saying "*As-Salamu 'Alaikum*" to Mr. Ahmad.

Isma'il sits in his seat. He keeps his desk very clean. He likes to read in his class. Ismail's friend Aisha asks him if she can borrow his book to read. Isma'il likes to share his things with others.

Mr. Ahmad tells the class that the school has decided to give an award to a student in the class who is responsible.

Mr. Ahmad says, "Isma'il is a very responsible boy. He always finishes his work on time. He does not hurt anyone's feelings. He shares his things with everyone. He helps everyone. He always gets very good grades. I am going to give Isma'il the best student award."

All the children in the class like Isma'il very much. They are very happy with the news. All of them congratulate Isma'il for winning the award.

WE HAVE LEARNED

- A Muslim is a responsible person.
- We should be responsible for what we say and do.
- We should be responsible to our family and others.
- We should be responsible for our schoolwork.

DO YOU KNOW THESE WORDS?
- responsible
- grades
- congratulate
- award

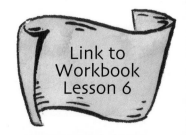
Link to Workbook Lesson 6

THINK ABOUT IT

Being Responsible For Our Words and Actions

We must be responsible for our words and actions. As Muslims, we should try to follow Prophet Muhammad ﷺ in our actions and thoughts. Prophet Muhammad ﷺ is the best example for us.

Read the following sentences in the boxes under '**CAUSE**'. Think of the effects to the causes that show a responsible Muslim. Write down your answers in the boxes under '**EFFECT**'. The first example is done for you.

CAUSE

Ahmad accidentally broke his neighbor's window during a soccer game.

Nuha had promised to help her mother to prepare dinner when Aishah asked her out to watch a movie.

Anwar's favourite TV program has started but he has not performed his *Salah*.

EFFECT

Ahmad stopped the game and said sorry to his neighbor for breaking the window.

_____
_____
_____
_____

_____
_____
_____
_____

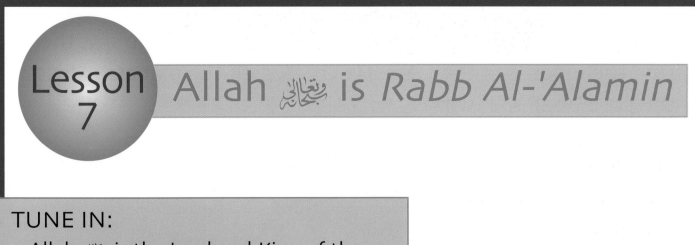

Lesson 7 — Allah ﷻ is Rabb Al-'Alamin

TUNE IN:

• Allah ﷻ is the Lord and King of the worlds. He is *Rabb Al-'Alamin*. Do you know what *Rabb Al-'Alamin* means?

Muslims believe that there is no god but Allah ﷻ. He is One and nothing is like Him.

He has always been there and He shall always be there. He created everything and no one created Him. He has no wife, son or daughter.

Allah ﷻ gave us families. We need our families. But Allah ﷻ does not need a family. He created us. He supports us in our life. We belong to Allah ﷻ. We will return to Him.

21

Allah ﷻ created this beautiful earth. He created the sky, the sun, the moon and the stars. He created all the planets. He is the Lord of all the worlds.

Allah ﷻ makes the trees grow. He makes the flowers bloom. He makes the fruits ripen. He made the wind, He made the clouds. He makes the rain and the snow. Allah ﷻ created this beautiful world for us. He is the only Lord.

Allah ﷻ is the *"Rabb"* of everyone. *"Rabb"* means the Lord and the King. He is the Lord and King of the worlds. We say He is *Rabb Al-'Alamin*. Everything follows His orders.

WE HAVE LEARNED

- There is only one God, Allah ﷻ.
- Allah ﷻ created everything.
- Allah ﷻ is the Lord and the King of the worlds.
- Allah ﷻ is the *Rabb Al-'Alamin*.
- We belong to Allah ﷻ and to Him we will return.

DO YOU KNOW THESE WORDS?
- Lord
- *Rabb al-'Alamin*
- oceans
- planets
- rivers

Link to Workbook Lesson 7

Allah ﷾ has Beautiful Names

- Allah ﷾ has many Beautiful Names. Let us learn some of them now!

Allah ﷾ has Beautiful Names. We can not see Allah ﷾, but we can learn about Him from His Beautiful Names.

WHO KNOWS EVERY THING?

Allah ﷻ is *Al-'Alim*. He is All-Knowing. He knows everything. He even knows what is in our hearts and in our minds.

WHO SEES EVERY ONE AND EVERY THING ?

Allah ﷻ is also *Al-Basir*. He sees everything. We cannot hide anything from Allah ﷻ. He is everywhere. He sees everything we do.

WHO HEARS EVERY WORD?

Allah ﷻ is also *As-Sami'*. He hears everyone. He can hear every word we say. He hears us even when we say things in our hearts. We can not hide anything from Him.

When we ask something from Him, He listens and accepts our *Du'a*.

LET US MAKE ALLAH ﷻ HAPPY!

Let us think of Allah ﷻ all the time.
Let us use only those words which He likes to hear.
Let us do only what He wants us to do.
Let us make Allah ﷻ happy with us.

Allah ﷻ is very close to us.
When we ask for His help, He helps us.

We must always remember Allah ﷻ.
We must worship Allah ﷻ alone.
We must ask for only Allah's help.

We come from Allah ﷻ, we belong to Him and we will return to Him.

WE HAVE LEARNED
- Allah is *Al-'Alim*. He is All-Knowing.
- Allah is *Al-Basir*. He sees everything.
- Allah is *As-Sami*. He hears everything.

DO YOU KNOW THESE WORDS?
- *Al-'Alim*
- *Al-Basir*
- *As-Sami*

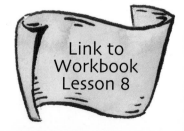

Link to
Workbook
Lesson 8

Allah's *Khalifah*

TUNE IN:

• I am Allah's *Khalifah* on earth. Allah ﷻ wants me to take good care of everyone and everything on earth.

Allah ﷻ created the worlds, the Angels and the Jinns. He created Prophet Adam ﷻ, the first man. He also created Hawwa ﷻ, wife of Adam, the first woman.

Allah ﷻ gave Prophet Adam ﷻ a mind to think and choose. He gave him a heart to feel and love. He also gave Hawwa ﷻ a mind and a heart.

Prophet Adam ﷻ and Hawwa ﷻ were very special creations of Allah ﷻ. He sent them to earth and gave them many children. Their children had many more children.

We are all children of Prophet Adam ﷺ and Hawa ﷺ. Allah ﷻ gave us a mind to think, learn and choose. He gave us a heart to feel and love. He gave us the power to choose what we say and what we do.

This is a big responsibility. He made us His *Khalifah* on earth. *Khalifah* means someone who follows Allah's commands and takes care of everything created by Allah ﷻ.

Khalifah takes care of others. Allah ﷻ wants us to take care of this world. He wants us to live in peace with each other. When we live in peace we help each other. We do not fight or make fun of others.

Allah ﷻ also wants us to take care of this beautiful earth. We should keep it clean. We should keep the rivers and oceans clean and save the environment.

As Allah's *Khalifah*, we must always follow His commands.

WE HAVE LEARNED

- We are the children of Prophet Adam ﷺ and Hawwa ﷻ, the first man and woman created by Allah ﷻ.
- Allah ﷻ made human beings His *Khalifah* on earth.
- Allah ﷻ gave us minds to think, heart to feel and love and the ability to choose.
- We must follow Allah's commands and take care of His earth.

DO YOU KNOW THESE WORDS?
- responsibility
- *Khalifah*
- environment

Link to Workbook Lesson 9

TUNE IN:

• There are FIVE pillars of Islam. Do you know what are these?

Allah ﷻ told us five special ways to be close to Him and keep away from *Shaitan*. These five actions are also called the "Five Pillars of Islam". Just like the pillars, these acts of *'Ibadah* helps us to be strong in our *Din*.

اَلشَّهَادَةُ

The first pillar is the *Shahadah*. All Muslims believe that Allah ﷻ is One and the Creator of all. Allah ﷻ sent many prophets to the world. Muhammad ﷺ is His last messenger and prophet.

اَلْأَحَدُ

We also believe that Allah ﷻ gave His Books to some of the prophets. He created the angels. Angels pray to Him all the time. Allah ﷻ has the power to know everything. Nothing can happen without his permission. This Power of Allah ﷻ is called *al-Qadr*.

اَلْقَدَرُ

Muslims believe that there is another life after death and we will return to Allah ﷻ. We do what Allah ﷻ wants us to do. Prophet Muhammad ﷺ has shown us how to live like a good Muslim.

All Muslims are required to live and act in a special way. We must say the *Shahadah* with our tongues and believe it in our hearts.

Muslims must pray five times a day. We must give *Zakah* to the poor and the needy. We fast in the month of *Ramadan*. We go to Makkah for *Hajj*, once in our life time.

Muslims must do these five acts of *Ibadah* to make Allah ﷻ happy. These are important acts of a Muslim. These acts are also called the five pillars of Islam.

WE HAVE LEARNED

- Every Muslim must believe in Allah ﷾, the Prophets of Allah, the Books of Allah ﷾, the angels, *al-Qadr* and life after death.
- There are five pillars of Islam: *Shahadah*, *Salah*, fasting, *Zakah* and *Hajj*.
- Muslims must follow the five acts of ʿ*Ibadah*.

DO YOU KNOW THESE WORDS?
- *Ibadah*
- *Al-Qadr*
- special
- required

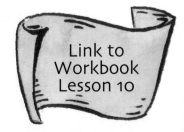

Link to Workbook Lesson 10

أَشْهَدُ أَنْ لاَ إِلَهَ إِلاَّ اللهُ ، وَحْدَهُ لاَ شَرِيكَ لَهُ ،
وَأَشْهَدُ أَنَّ مُحَمَّدًا عَبْدُهُ وَرَسُولُهُ .

"I bear witness that here is no god but Allah,
And I bear witness that Muhammad
is the Messenger of Allah."

Shahadah means "to be a witness". Anyone who makes this *Shahadah* and believes in it is called a Muslim. We cannot be a Muslim unless we say the *Shahadah* and believe it in our hearts.

The word *Islam* comes from the Arabic word *Salima*, which means 'peace'. This means that Islam is a way of peace.

اَلسَّلاَمُ

The word Islam also comes from Arabic word *Aslama*, which means "to obey". This means that Muslims always obey Allah ﷻ. Allah ﷻ says in the Qur'an:

$$\text{وَأَطِيعُواْ ٱللَّهَ وَٱلرَّسُولَ لَعَلَّكُمْ تُرْحَمُونَ}$$

"And obey Allah and Messenger, so that you might receive Mercy."
(*Al-'Imran 3: 132*)

WHO IS A MUSLIM?

A Muslim is one who believes in Islam and follows it. A Muslim knows Allah ﷻ is his Lord and Creator. A Muslim is one who follows the teachings of the Qur'an. A Muslim is one who follows Prophet Muhammad ﷺ as the final Prophet and Messenger.

WE BELONG TO MUSLIM *UMMAH*

All Muslims belong to one *Ummah,* which means a community or a nation. All Muslims have the same beliefs and all of them follow the teachings of Islam.

Muslims live all over the world.

All Muslims are brothers and sisters to one another. All Muslims are equal before Allah ﷻ. No one among them is better than other because of language or race. The Qur'an says:

إِنَّ أَكْرَمَكُمْ عِندَاللَّهِ أَتْقَكُمْ

"The best in the eyes of Allah is one who is most pious."
(Al-Hujurat 49:13)

We thank Allah ﷻ for giving us Islam. We thank Him for sending us His book, the Qur'an. We thank Allah ﷻ for choosing us to be in the *Ummah* of Prophet Muhammad ﷺ.

WE HAVE LEARNED

- Islam means a religion of peace and obedience to Allah ﷻ.
- A Muslim is one who believes in Islam and follows it.
- All Muslims are one *Ummah*. We are brothers and sisters to each other.

DO YOU KNOW THESE WORDS?
- *Salima-*(Peace)
- *Aslama*-(To obey)
- witness
- community -(ummah)
- nation

Link to Workbook Lesson 11

Salah: A Special Gift from Allah سبحانه وتعالى

TUNE IN:

- "*Salah* is the key to *Jannah*"
  (Ibn Ahmad, Ibn Majah)
  Salah brings us closer to Allah سبحانه وتعالى.

Salah is the Islamic word for prayer. It is a gift of Allah سبحانه وتعالى to the Muslims. *Salah* keeps us away from many wrong thoughts and actions.

Allah سبحانه وتعالى gave us the power to choose what we think and do. Sometimes we forget and choose to do things which are harmful to us and to other people, like stealing, yelling at people or telling lies. Such actions are not liked by Allah سبحانه وتعالى.

When we stand in peace to make *Salah*, we think of Allah ﷻ. We think of our duties to Him. We think of our wrong actions and ask Allah ﷻ to forgive us. Thus, *Salah* is a reminder for us to always choose to do the right action and make Allah ﷻ happy with us.

Allah ﷻ asked us to make *Salah* five times each day. We have to make each *Salah* at a special time. We cannot make the five daily *Salawat* any time we want to. It is important to make each *Salah* at the fixed times.

إِنَّ ٱلصَّلَوٰةَ كَانَتْ عَلَى ٱلْمُؤْمِنِينَ كِتَٰبًا مَّوْقُوتًا

"The *Salah* is made obligatory for the Believers
to be made at fixed times."
(An-Nisa': 103)

Sometimes we think we are too busy to stop and make *Salah*. But nobody was busier than Prophet Muhammad ﷺ was. He had to take care of his family and everyone else. He was a teacher, a ruler and a prophet. But he never missed his prayer. He even used to pray many extra prayers.

THE WISDOM OF
OUR PROPHET ﷺ

Once Prophet Muhammad ﷺ asked the people sitting around him, "If there was a river at your door and you took a bath in it five times a day, would there be any dirt left on you?"
The *Sahabah* answered, " No."
Then the Prophet ﷺ said, " It is just like the five daily prayers which Allah uses to clean bad deeds
(Bukhari , Muslim)

WE HAVE LEARNED
- The *Salah* is an obligation for every Muslim.
- Prophet Muhammad ﷺ set the best example for us for the performance of the *Salah*.
- We show our obedience to Allah ﷻ through the *Salah*.

DO YOU KNOW THESE WORDS?
- obligation
- *Fard*
- worship
- obedience
- peace

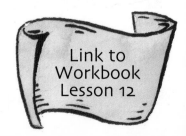
Link to
Workbook
Lesson 12

When we wish to please and obey Allah ﷻ, we make *Salah*. *Salah* makes us very near and close to Allah ﷻ. Let us find out the cause and effect relationship between our *Ibadah* and pleasure of Allah ﷻ.

Read the following sentences in the boxes under '**CAUSE**'. Think of the correct responses for the causes that a Muslim should display in the relationship between pleasing and obeying Allah ﷻ and offering *Salah*. Write down your answers in the boxes under '**EFFECT**'. The first example is done for you.

CAUSE

EFFECT

We love Allah ﷻ and want to make Him happy

→ We make *Salah* five times each day

Allah ﷻ wants us to be clean and pure before *salah*

→ _____

Allah ﷻ says in the Qur'an, "Call on me; I will answer your (prayer)." (Ghafir: 60)

→ _____

TUNE IN:

- *Salah* is a very special activity. We need to do many things before we begin to pray. Let us see if you know them.

BEING CLOSER TO ALLAH ﷻ

Salah brings us closer to Allah ﷻ. When we pray we are standing before Allah ﷻ. We cannot see Him, but He sees us. We feel closer to Him. We pray because Allah ﷻ has asked us to "establish *Salah*".

WE GET CLEAN AND WELL DRESSED FOR *SALAH*

Salah time is our special time with Allah ﷻ. It is like getting ready for a meeting. When we go to meet our principal or teacher we take a shower and wear nice clean clothes. We do not go to any meeting dirty. We do not go to a meeting half dressed.

Think about it! When we stand up for *Salah*, we are standing in front of Allah ﷾, the Lord and the Creator of the world. How can we stand in front of Him unclean and improperly dressed?

It is important that we get properly ready for *Salah*. This means that we make our bodies clean and wear clean clothes. The clothes should cover our bodies well. Prophet Muhammad ﷺ has said;

مِفْتَاحُ الصَّلاَةِ الطُّهُور .....

The key to *Salah* is being clean".
(Musnad Ahmad)

We wash ourselves in a special way before we make *Salah*. This is called *Wudu*. Prophet Muhammad ﷺ had shown us how to make *Wudu*. We will learn how to make *Wudu* in the next lesson.

We should also wear clean clothes. We should wear the clothes which cover our bodies well. The place we stand to offer *Salah* should also be very clean. We can spread a clean prayer rug or a sheet and stand on it for *Salah*.

WE HAVE LEARNED

- *Salah* brings us closer to Allah ﷾.
- We should make *Wudu* before we stand up to offer *Salah*.
- We should also wear clean clothes which cover our bodies well when we pray.

DO YOU KNOW THESE WORDS?
- closer
- *Wudu*
- dressed
- sheet

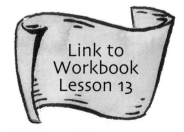

Link to Workbook Lesson 13

Making *Wudu*

TUNE IN:

- Do you know that Muslims make a special washing before their prayers?

THIS IS HOW WE MAKE *WUDU*

We make *Wudu* with clean and pure water. We wash certain parts of the body. Some of the parts are washed three times.

Prophet Muhammad ﷺ showed us how to make *Wudu*. We should make *Wudu* in the same way he did.

Let us recall the steps of making *Wudu*.

Before we begin to make *Wudu*, we make the intention for *Wudu*. We may say the intention in Arabic or in our own language.

نَوَيْتُ أَنْ أَتَوَضَّأَ لِلصَّلاَةِ

"I have the intention to make *Wudu* for Allah, the High."

We begin with *Bismillah* and start making *Wudu*. We say:

بِسْمِ اللَّهِ الرَّحْمَنِ الرَّحِيْمِ

"In the name of Allah, Most Gracious, Most Merciful."

1. We wash our hands up to the wrists. (3 times)

2. We rinse our mouth with water. (3 times)

3. We wash our nose. (3 times)

4. We wash our face from the forehead to the chin and from ear to ear. (3 times)

5. We wash our arms up to the elbow, first right arm and then left. (3 times)

6. We wet our hands with water; wipe our head starting from the forehead and over to the back of the head.

7. We clean our ears. We pass wet thumbs behind the ear from the top of the ear to the lobe.

8. We wash our feet up to the ankle; first, the right foot and then the left foot.

It is important for us to follow proper order in making *Wudu*.

It is *Sunnah* for us to say the *Du'a* when we are done making *Wudu*. We have learned the *Du'a* in Grade One. Can you recite the *Du'a* together with your friends?

WE HAVE LEARNED

- *Wudu* is required before *Salah*.
- We must follow the proper order in making *Wudu*.
- It is *Sunnah* for us to read the *Du'a* after making the *Wudu*.

DO YOU KNOW THESE WORDS?
- purity
- intention
- recite
- cleanliness
- rinse

Link to Workbook Lesson 14

TUNE IN:

- Do you know that when we hear the *Adhan* we have to respond to it? Let us learn how to respond to the *Adhan*.

Today Uncle Ahmad is teaching the boys how to make the *Adhan*. The *Adhan* must be called for each *Salah* to invite people to prayer. It is a *Sunnah* to hear the *Adhan* and respond to the call of the *Adhan*.

The *Mu'adhin* stands up facing the *Qiblah* and calls the *Adhan*.

When we hear the *Adhan*, we must stop talking. We should listen to the *Adhan* and answer it.

Making the *Adhan* and responding to the *Adhan*.

THE *ADHAN*

THE RESPONSE

1.

اَللَّهُ أَكْبَرُ ، اَللَّهُ أَكْبَرُ

Allah is Greatest!

اَللَّهُ أَكْبَرُ ، اللهُ أَكْبَرُ

Allah is Greatest!

2.

أَشْهَدُ أَنْ لَا إِلَهَ إِلاَّ اَللَّهُ

I bear witness that there is no god but Allah

أَشْهَدُ أَنْ لَا إِلَهَ إِلاَّ اَللَّهُ

I bear witness that there is no god but Allah

3.

أَشْهَدُ أَنَّ مُحَمَّدًا رَسُولُ اللَّهِ

I bear witness that Muhammad is the Messenger of Allah

أَشْهَدُ أَنَّ مُحَمَّدًا رَسُولُ اللَّهِ

I bear witness that Muhammad is the Messenger of Allah

4.

حَيَّ عَلَى الصَّلاَةِ

Come to the *Salah*

لاَ حَوْلَ وَلاَ قُوَّةَ إِلاَّ بِاللَّهِ

There is no force and no power, except the Power of Allah.

47

THE *ADHAN*	THE RESPONSE

5.

حَيَّ عَلَى الْفَلاَحِ

Come to the Success.

لاَ حَوْلَ وَلاَ قُوَّةَ إِلاَّ بِاللَّهِ

There is no force and no power, except the Power of Allah.

6.

اللَّهُ أَكْبَرُ ، اللَّهُ أَكْبَرُ

Allah is Greatest!

اَللَّهُ أَكْبَرُ ، اللَّهُ أَكْبَرُ

Allah is Greatest!

7.

لاَ إِلَهَ إِلاَّ اللَّهُ

There is no god but Allah.

لاَ إِلَهَ إِلاَّ اللَّهُ

There is no god but Allah.

In the *Fajr* prayer, after we read:

"*Hayya 'Alal-Falah*",
"Come to success"

We add the following:

اَلصَّلاةُ خَيْرٌ مِنَ النَّوْمِ

Prayer is better than sleep.

LET US GO TO THE *MASJID*!

When we hear the *Adhan*, we should make *Wudu* and go to the *Masjid*. We go to *Masjid* to offer *Salah* in *Jama'ah* with other Muslims. If we live close to a *Masjid* we should always offer *Salah* in the *Masjid*.

If we cannot go to the *Masjid*, then we should make *Wudu* and make *Salah* at home.

After a short time, the *Mu'adhin* says the following:

"For sure the time for *Salah* has arrived"

When we hear these words in the *Masjid*, we must all stand up for the *Salah*. We must stand in straight rows, shoulder to shoulder, facing the *Qiblah* and behind the *Imam*.

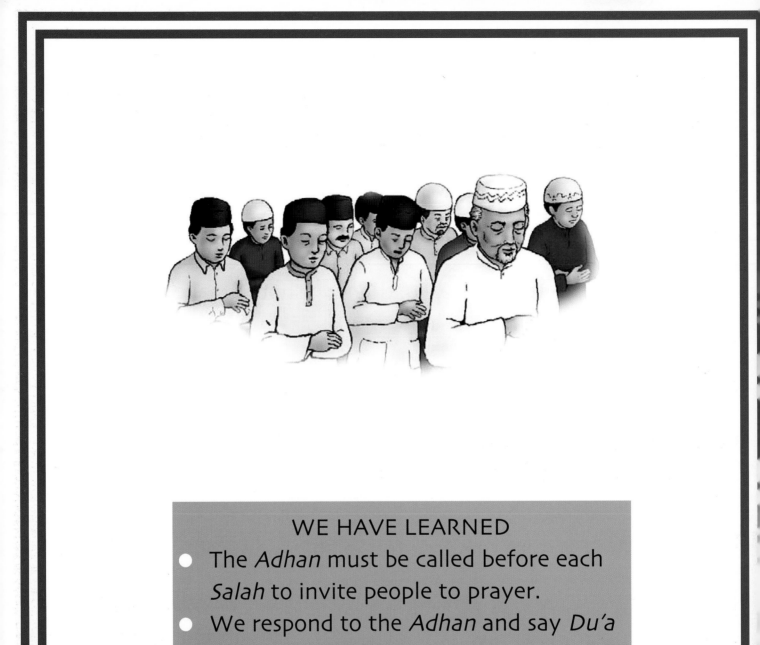

WE HAVE LEARNED

- The *Adhan* must be called before each *Salah* to invite people to prayer.
- We respond to the *Adhan* and say *Du'a* after the *Adhan*.
- The *Iqamah* is called to invite people to stand up for *Salah*.

DO YOU KNOW THESE WORDS?
- *Adhan*
- *Qiblah*
- *Iqamah*
- *Mu'adhin*

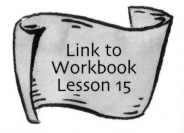

Link to Workbook Lesson 15

TUNE IN:

- Allah ﷻ has asked us to pray five times a day. Prophet Muhammad ﷺ has shown us how to get ready for *Salah*. He has also shown us how to say the *Salah*. Let us do our *Salah* as taught by Prophet Muhammad ﷺ.

- "*Niyyah, Qiyam, Ruku, Qawmah, Sajdah, Jalsah and Salam*". Do you know these words? Let us find out!

Every *Salah* has units. They are called *Raka'at*. Each *Raka'h* is very much like the others, with small differences. Each *Salah* has two, three or four *Raka'at*.

A *Salah* may be *Fard*, *Sunnah* or *Nafl*. Let us learn to make *Fard Salah* first.

HOW TO MAKE TWO *RAKA'AT FARD* *FAJR SALAH*

Making the Intention (*Niyyah*)

We stand up on a clean prayer rug or carpet. We face the *Qiblah*. And make the intention for the *Salah*. It is important to make the intention for the *Salah*.

For example when we want to offer two *Raka'at Fard Salah* at *Fajr* time, we say:

"I intend to perform the *Salah* of Fajr.
Two *Raka'at Fard*.
For the sake of Allah ﷻ.
My face is turned towards the Ka'bah."

If we are offering the two *Raka'at Fajr Salah* with *Jama'ah*, we will say:

"I intend to perform the *Salah* of *Fajr*.
Two *Raka'at Fard*.
For the sake of Allah ﷻ.
My face is turned towards the *Ka'bah*.
Behind the *Imam*."

FIRST *RAK'AH*

After the intention, we raise our hands up to our ears and say "*Allahu Akbar*", and fold them in front of us, right hand over the left hand.

I. *QIYAM*: STANDING

1. We stand up straight , facing the *Qiblah* our hands folded in front of us. If we are praying in *Jama'ah*, then we follow the *Imam*.

2. Recite *Thana* quietly

> *Subhanaka 'Allahumma*
>
> *Wa bi-hamdi-ka*
>
> *Wa tabarak-'Asmu-ka*
>
> *Wa ta'la jaddu-ka*
>
> *Wa la ilaha ghairu-ka*

سُبْحَانَكَ اللَّهُمَّ
وَبِحَمْدِكَ ،
وَتَبَارَكَ اسْمُكَ ،
وَتَعَالَى جَدُّكَ ،
وَلاَ إِلَهَ غَيْرُكَ

All Glory be to you, O Allah
And praises are for you.
And Blessed is Your Name.
And You are high.
And there is no god except You.

3. Recite *Tasmiyah* and *Surah Al-Fatihah* quietly.

If we are following the *Imam*, then he recites *Tasmiyah* and *Surah Al-Fatihah* aloud and we listen quietly.

1. Bismillahi-r-Rahman-ir-Rahim.
2. Al-hamdu lillahi Rabbi-l-'alamin.
3. Ar-Rahmani-r-Rahim.
4. Maliki Yawmi-d-din.
5. Iyyaka na'budu wa iyyaka nasta'in.
6. Ihdina-s-sirat-al mustaqim.
7. Sirat-al-ladhina 'an'amta 'alaihim Ghayri-l-maghdubi 'alaihim Wala-d-dalin, 'Amin

بِسْمِ ٱللَّهِ ٱلرَّحْمَـٰنِ ٱلرَّحِيمِ ﴿١﴾
ٱلْحَمْدُ لِلَّهِ رَبِّ ٱلْعَـٰلَمِينَ ﴿٢﴾
ٱلرَّحْمَـٰنِ ٱلرَّحِيمِ ﴿٣﴾
مَـٰلِكِ يَوْمِ ٱلدِّينِ ﴿٤﴾
إِيَّاكَ نَعْبُدُ وَإِيَّاكَ نَسْتَعِينُ ﴿٥﴾
ٱهْدِنَا ٱلصِّرَٰطَ ٱلْمُسْتَقِيمَ ﴿٦﴾
صِرَٰطَ ٱلَّذِينَ أَنْعَمْتَ عَلَيْهِمْ
غَيْرِ ٱلْمَغْضُوبِ عَلَيْهِمْ
وَلَا ٱلضَّآلِّينَ ﴿٧﴾

1. In the name of Allah, the Most Merciful, the Mercy Giving.
2. Praise be to Allah, Lord of the worlds.
3. Most Merciful, Most Kind.
4. Master of the Day of Judgment.
5. You alone we worship, You alone we ask for help.
6. Show us the Straight Path:
7. The Path of those whom You have favored,
   Not (the Path) of those, with whom You are angry,
   Nor of those who lose their way. Amin.

When the *Imam* finishes reciting
Surat ul-Fatihah, we say "*Amin*". If we are praying alone
then after *Surat ul-Fatihah*, we say *Amin*" also.

4. We recite a short *Surah* quietly. If we
    are praying in *Jama'ah*, then the
    'Imam recites a short *Surah*, or the
    Ayat of a long *Surah* aloud.

II. *RUKU* : BENDING DOWN

When praying alone, after short *Surah*, we say "*Allahu Akbar*"
and make a *Ruku*.

If praying in *Jama'ah* we follow the *Imam*.

After the recitation of the short *Surah* , the *Imam* says
"*Allahu Akbar*' and makes a *Ruku*, bowing from the waist,
with his hands on his knees.

We follow the *Imam*. Say "*Allahu Akbar*" quietly and bow from our waist, with our hands on our knees.

While in *Ruku*, we say silently, three times:

> *Subhana Rabbi-al ʿAzim*
> *Magnificent is my Lord, the Greatest*

سُبْحَانَ رَبِّيَ الْعَظِيم

III. *QAWMAH*: SHORT STANDING

We stand up saying:

> *Samiʿ Allahu li man hamidah*
> *Allah has heard the call of the one who has praised Him*

If we are praying in *Jama'ah* then, the *Imam* stands up saying:

> *Samiʿ Allahu li man hamidah*

سَمِعَ اللَّهُ لِمَنْ حَمِدَه

And we follow him saying:

> *Rabbana wa la ka-l-hamd*
> *Our Lord, and the praise is for You*

رَبَّنَا وَلَكَ الْحَمْد

IV. FIRST *SAJDAH*: FIRST PROSTRATION

1. Raising our hands to the ears we say "*Allahu Akbar*" and go into *Sajdah*. While in *Sajdah*, our forehead and nose should touch the floor. Palms of both hands should also be down touching the floor.

   If we are praying in *Jama'ah*, we follow the *Imam*. The *Imam* says, "*Allahu Akbar*" and goes into *Sajdah*. We follow him.

2. While in *Sajdah*, we say three times, silently:

   "*Subhana Rabbiya-l-'Ala*"
   Glorious is my Lord, the Highest.

   سُبْحَانَ رَبِّيَ الأَعْلَى

V. SHORT *JALSAH*: SHORT SITTING

We rise from the *Sajdah* saying "*Allahu Akbar*" and sit briefly.

If praying in *Jama'ah*, we follow the *Imam*.

VI. SECOND *SAJDAH*: SECOND PROSTRATION

1.   We say "*Allahu Akbar*" and make the second *Sajdah*, as before and say "*Subhana Rabbiya-l-'Ala*" three times.

If we are praying in *Jama'ah*, then we follow the *Imam*. The *Imam* says "*Allahu Akbar*" and makes a second *Sajdah*, just like the first one.

We follow the *Imam* and say "*Allahu Akbar*" quietly and go into *Sajdah* behind the *Imam*. We say "*Subhana Rabbiya-l-'Ala*" three times quietly.

We rise from the second *Sajdah*, saying "*Allahu Akbar*" and stand up for the second *Raka'ah*.

When praying in *Jama'ah*, we follow the *Imam* and stand up for the second *Raka'ah* with him.

This completes the first *Raka'ah*.

WE HAVE LEARNED

- We pray two *Raka'at Fard* for *Fajr Salah.*
- The first *Raka'ah* has *Niyyah, Qiyam, Ruku, Qaumah,* first *Sajdah*, short *Jalsah* and second *Sajdah.*
- When pray in *Jama'ah*, we follow the *Imam.*

DO YOU KNOW THESE WORDS?

- *Jalsah*
- *Qawmah*
- *Qiyam*
- *Ruku*
- *Sajdah*
- *Tasmiyah*
- *Raka' at*

Link to Workbook Lesson 16

TUNE IN:

- Now you know how to offer the first *Raka'ah* of two *Raka'at Fard Salah.* Let us learn to offer the second *Raka'ah* and complete the *Salah*

After completing the first *Raka'ah*, we stand up and begin the second *Raka'ah*.

I. *QIYAM*: STANDING

We do not begin the second *Raka'ah* with *Thana*. We start by reciting *Tasmiyah* and *Surat-ul-Fatihah*. Then, we recite another short *Surah* or *Ayat* from the Qur'an, just like we have done in the first *Raka'ah*.

If we are praying in *Jama'ah* , we follow the Imam. He recites the *Tasmiyah, Surat-ul-Fatiha* and a short *Surah* or *Ayat* from the Qur'an. We listen to the *Imam* quietly.

II. *RUKU*: BENDING DOWN

As in the first *Raka'ah*, in the second *Raka'ah* also, we bend down in *Ruku* saying "*Allahu Akbar*" and say "*Subhana Rabbi-al 'Azim*" quietly three times.

III. *QAWMAH*: SHORT STANDING

We stand up from the *Ruku* saying:

سَمِعَ اللَّهُ لِمَنْ حَمِدَه

"*Sami Allahu li man hamidah*"

If we are praying in *Jama'ah*, then we stand up following the *Imam*. The *Imam* says:

"*Sami Allahu li man hamidah*"   سَمِعَ اللَّهُ لِمَنْ حَمِدَه

And we say,

"*Rabbana wa la ka-l-hamd*".   رَبَّنَا وَلَكَ الْحَمْد

IV. FIRST *SAJDAH*: FIRST PROSTRATION

We raise our hands and our ears and say "Allahu Akbar" and go into *Sajdah*.

If we are following the *Imam*, then he says "Allahu Akbar" aloud and goes into *Sajdah*. We follow him.

While in *Sajdah*, we all say:

"Subhana Rabbiya-l-'Ala"
(three times).

سُبْحَانَ رَبِّيَ الْأَعْلَى

V. SHORT *JALSAH*: SHORT SITTING

We rise from *Sajdah*, saying "'Allahu Akbar" and sit for a very short time.

If we are behind the *Imam*, then we follow him. He rises from the *Sajdah*, saying "Allahu Akbar" and sits for a very short time.

VI. SECOND *SAJDAH*: SECOND PROSTRATION

We say "Allahu Akbar" and make a second *Sajdah*, just like the first one. While in *Sajdah*, we say:
"Subhana Rabbiya-l-'Ala"
(three times)

سُبْحَانَ رَبِّيَ الْأَعْلَى

VII. LONG *JALSAH*: LONG SITTING

In the second *Rak'ah*, we do not stand up after the second *Sajdah*. Instead we sit in a long *Jalsah* and say *At-Tashahhud; As-Salatu-l-Ibrahimiyyah* and *Taslim*.

AT-TASHAHHUD:

At-tahiyyatu lil-Lahi
Wa-s-salawatu wat tayyibatu
As-salamu 'alai-ka ayyuha-n-nabiyyu
Wa rahmatu-lahi wa barakatu-Hu
As-salamu 'alaina
Wa 'ala ibadilLahi-s-salihin
Ashhadu an la illaha illa-Laahu
Wa ashhadu anna Muhammadan
Abdu-Hu wa rasulu-Hu
(We raise the index finger of right hand when we say the last three lines of *At-Tashahhud*.)

اَلتَّحِيَّاتُ لِلَّه
وَالصَّلَوَاتُ وَالطَّيِّبَاتِ ،
اَلسَّلَامُ عَلَيْكَ أَيُّهَا النَّبِيُّ
وَرَحْمَةُ اللهِ وَبَرَكَاتُهُ ،
اَلسَّلَامُ عَلَيْنَا
وَعَلَى عِبَادِ اللهِ الصَّالِحِينَ ،
أَشْهَدُ أَنْ لاَ إِلَهَ إِلاَّ اللهُ ،
وَأَشْهَدُ أَنَّ مُحَمَّدًا
عَبْدُهُ وَرَسُولُهُ .

All the praises, prayers and good things are for Allah. O Prophet! Peace be upon you and His Mercy and His Blessings. Peace be upon us and upon the pious servants of Allah. I bear witness that there is no god but Allah and that Muhammad is His servant and His messenger.

After *At-Tashahhud* we recite *As Salatu-l-Ibrahimiyyah*.

Allahumma salli 'ala Muhammadin
wa 'ala ali Muhammadin
Kama sallaita 'ala Ibrahima
Wa 'ala ali Ibrahima
Inna-Ka Hamidum Majid
Allahumma barik 'ala Muhammadin
Wa 'ala ali Muhammadin
Kama barakta 'ala Ibrahima
Wa 'ala ali Ibrahima
Inna-Ka Hamidum Majid

اَللّٰهُمَّ صَلِّ عَلَى مُحَمَّدٍ ،
وَعَلَى آلِ مُحَمَّدٍ ،
كَمَا صَلَّيْتَ عَلَى إِبْرَاهِيمَ ،
وَعَلَى آلِ إِبْرَاهِيمَ ،
إِنَّكَ حَمِيدٌ مَجِيدٌ .
اَللّٰهُمَّ بَارِكْ عَلَى مُحَمَّدٍ ،
وَعَلَى آلِ مُحَمَّدٍ ،
كَمَا بَارَكْتَ عَلَى إِبْرَاهِيمَ ،
وَعَلَى آلِ إِبْرَاهِيمَ ،
إِنَّكَ حَمِيدٌ مَجِيدٌ .

O Allah, greet Muhammad and the family of Muhammad as You have greeted Ibrahim and the family of Ibrahim. Indeed! You are the Glorious Praised One.
O Allah, bless Muhammad and the family of Muhammad as You have blessed Ibrahim and the family of Ibrahim. Indeed! You are the Glorious Praised One.

After saying *Salatu-l-Ibrahimiyyah* we turn face towards the right and say *Taslim*:

اَلسَّلاَمُ عَلَيْكُمْ وَرَحْمَةُ اللَّهِ ،

"As-salamu 'Alaikum wa Rahmatullah"
The Peace and Mercy of Allah be upon you.

Then, we turn our face to the left and say *Taslim*:

اَلسَّلاَمُ عَلَيْكُمْ وَرَحْمَةُ اللَّه ،

"*As-salamau 'Alaikum wa Rahmatullah*"
The Peace and Mercy of Allah be upon you.

When we pray in *Jama'ah*, we follow the
Imam and say *Taslim* after him.
This completes the two *Raka'ah Salah Fard*.

WE HAVE LEARNED

- We sit for a long second *Jalsah*
- In the second *Jalsah*, we say *At-Tashahhud*, *As-Salatu-l-Ibrahimiyyah* and *Taslim*

DO YOU KNOW THESE WORDS?
- *At-Tahiyyat*
- *taslim*
- blessings
- *As-Salatu-l-'Ibrahimiyya*

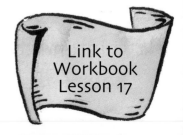

Link to
Workbook
Lesson 17

Making Four *Raka'at* of *Fard Salah*

TUNE IN:

• How many *Raka'at* of *Fard Salah* are there in *Zuhr*, *'Asr*, *Maghrib* and *'Isha* Prayers?
Let us find out!

When we offer the *Fard Salawat* of *Zuhr*, *Asr* and *Isha*, we pray **four** *Raka'at*. Maghrib *Salah* has only **three** *Fard Raka'at*.

The first two *Raka'at* of the four *Raka'at Salah* are almost offered the same way as in *Fajr Salah*. However, there is a difference. Let us learn it now!

FIRST *RAKA'AH*

We take the following steps:

1. Intention (*Niyyah*)
   We follow the same steps in making the intention for the four *Raka'at Fard Salah* as for the two *Raka'at* except in the beginning we say:

   "I intend to perform the *Zuhr Salah* ('Asr or 'Isha), Four *Raka'at Fard*."

Each one of the following steps of the first *Raka'ah* are performed the same way as in the first *Raka'ah* of Two *Raka'at Fajr* prayer:

QIYAM: Standing

RUKU: Bending Down

QAWMAH: Short Standing

FIRST *SAJDAH*: First Prostration

SHORT *JALSAH*: Short Sitting

SECOND *SAJDAH*: Second Prostration

After completing first *Raka'ah*, we stand up and begin the second *Raka'ah*.

SECOND *RAKA'AH*

We follow the same steps as in the second *Raka'ah* of two *Raka'at Fard salah* except for the LONG *JALSAH*:

QIYAM

RUKU

QAWMAH

FIRST *SAJDAH*

SHORT *JALSAH*

SECOND *SAJDAH*

LONG JALSAH: We sit in the long *Jalsah* and recite *At-Tashahhud.* We do not recite *Salatu-l-Ibrahimiyyah* or *Taslim.* But stand up for the third *Qiyam.*

THIRD *RAKA'AH*

After *At-Tashahhud* we stand up in *Qiyam* again.

QIYAM- STANDING: We Say *Tasmiyah* and *Al-Fatihah* but do not recite a short *Surah*.

Rest of the steps:

Ruku, Qawmah, first *Sajdah*, short *Jalsah* and second *Sajdah*, we do the same way as in the first *Raka'ah*.

After second *Sajdah*, we stand up in *Qiyam* saying *Allahu Akbar*. Now we begin the fourth and the last *Raka'ah* of the four *Raka'at Fard Salah*.

FOURTH *RAKA'AH*

QIYAM – STANDING: We say *Tasmiyah* and *Al-Fatihah* but do not recite a short *Surah*. Then we perform the following steps:

Ruku', Qawmah, first *Sajdah*, short *Jalsah* and second *Sajdah*

LONG *JALSAH:* we sit in the long *Jalsah* and recite *At-Tashahhud* and *Salatu-l-Ibrahimiyyah*. Then we say the *Taslim*.

This completes the four *Raka'at Fard Salah*.

COMPLETING THE THREE *RAKA'AT* OF *MAGHRIB SALAH*:

In *Maghrib* Salah we follow the same steps as in the third *Raka'ah* of four *Fard Salah*, except that after second *Sajdah*, we sit in a long *Jalsah* and complete the *Salah*.
We follow the following steps:

> THIRD *RAKA'AH*
> > *Qiyam*
> > *Qawmah*
> > *Ruku*
> > First *Sajdah*
> > Short *Jalsah*
> > Second *Sajdah*
> > Long *Jalsah*: We sit in the long *Jalsah*. Recite *At-Tashahhud, Salatu-l-Ibrahimiyyah* and *Taslim*.

This completes three *Raka'at* of *Fard Maghrib salah*.

WE HAVE LEARNED
- We pray four *Raka'at Fard* for *Zuhr, 'Asr* and *Isha* prayers.
- In third and fourth *Raka'at* of *Fard salawat*, we do not recite a short *Surah* after *Al -Fatihah*.
- *Maghrib Salah* has three *Fard Raka'at*.

DO YOU KNOW THESE WORDS?
- *At-Tashahhud*
- *Amin*
- *Salatu-l-Ibrahimiyyah*

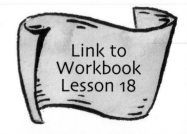
Link to Workbook Lesson 18

Sawm: Fasting in the Month of *Ramadan*

TUNE IN:

- *Sawm* is an Arabic word. It means "Giving up". What do you think we give up when we fast? Think about it!

Allah ﷻ made fasting *Fard* in the month of *Ramadan* for all Muslims. We begin to fast when we see the new moon of *Ramadan.*

Ramadan is the ninth month of the Islamic calendar. We fast every day for 29 or 30 days. We stop fasting when we see the new moon of the month of *Shawwal.*

Muslims do not eat or drink anything from dawn to sunset every day for the whole month. Except for young children, old people, sick people and the people who are travelling.

WHY DO WE FAST?

We fast for Allah ﷻ. We fast because He asks us to fast. We want to make Allah ﷻ happy by obeying Him.

When we fast we think of Allah ﷻ. It keeps our hearts and minds pure. We try to remember Allah ﷻ and read as much Qur'an as we can.

We should be careful not to say wrong words, especially in *Ramadan.* It may hurt someone's feelings. We should not listen to people who are using bad language. We should not fight or hurt anyone with our hands.

SUHUR: We begin the fast with *Suhur.* This is the meal we eat just before dawn. It is important for us to eat at *Suhur* time. It gives us energy for the rest of the day of fasting. It is also a *Sunnah* of our dear Prophet ﷺ.

Intention to Fast:

It is important to make our intention to fast every morning. We make this intention after we finish eating *Suhur,* before dawn.

We say the following *Du'a* and make our intention:

نَوَيْتُ أَنْ أَصُومَ لِلَّهِ تَعَالَى غَدًا مِنْ شَهْرِ رَمَضَان

"I intend to fast, for the sake of Allah, the Most High, tommorrow during the month of Ramadan."

IFTAR: In the evening, after sunset, we break the fast. This time is called *Iftar*. We sit together with our family and friends and break the fast with dates. It is *Sunnah* to break the fast with dates. If we do not have dates we can break the fast with any healthy food. We say this *Du'a* just before we begin to eat:

اللَّهُمَّ لَكَ صُمْتُ ، وَعَلَى رِزْقِكَ أَفْطَرْت

"O Allah! For You I have fasted, and on Your provisions I have broken my fast".

TARAWIH SALAH:

We finish our day of fasting by making the *Tarawih Salah* at night after 'Isha prayers. *Tarawih Salah* is a *Sunnah*. We can offer *Tarawih Salah* at home. But it feels very good to offer it with other Muslims behind an *Imam* in the *Masjid*. Usually, the *Imam* is a *Hafiz*, who recites the whole Qur'an over the month.

The blessed month of *Ramadan* ends when we see the moon of *Shawwal*. Next day we celebrate the '*Id –ul-Fitr* and thank Allah ﷻ for giving us the blessed month of *Ramadan*.

WE HAVE LEARNED
- The month of *Ramadan* is the ninth month of the Islamic Calendar.
- All healthy adult Muslims must fast every day in the month of *Ramadan*.
- Muslims fast from dawn to sunset.
- Muslims spend their time fasting reading the Qur'an and doing good deeds.
- *Tarawih* are special prayers, offered after '*Isha* in *Ramadan*.

DO YOU KNOW THESE WORDS?
- Calendar
- Suhur
- dawn
- Iftar
- Sawm
- Tarawih

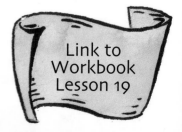
Link to Workbook Lesson 19

We are Muslims. We have responsibilities towards Allah ﷾, such as praying to Him and keeping fast for Him.

We also have certain responsibilities towards other human beings. Taking care of the poor and needy with our money is one of those responsibilities. It is *Fard* on every adult Muslim who has enough money to give some of his or her money to another Muslim who does not have enough. This kind of sharing is called *Zakat*.

Zakat is an important pillar of Islam. It is a *Fard* just like *Salah* and *Saum.* Muslims who have saved enough money must give 2.5% of it to poor and needy Muslims every year.

Zakat is an Arabic word. It mans "To make clean and pure". When we give some of our money away for Allah ﷻ, the rest of it becomes clean and pure. It gets clean from selfishness. We learn sharing and caring. We stop being selfish.

زَكَاة

Zakat makes us pure because it brings Allah's blessings to us. He is happy with us when we obey Him. He likes it when we share with our needy brothers and sisters. When we share our wealth with those who do not have any, we get rid of greed. We become generous.

Let us not forget that everything we have is given to us by Allah ﷻ. It is Allah's wealth. He can take it away any time He wants to. So, when we give some of it to the needy people, we are giving from Allah's wealth.

Zakat is *Fard* on every Muslim who:

1. has more wealth than he or she needs.
2. has had the wealth for at least a year.
3. does not owe money to anyone.
4. is an adult
5. is sane

Many Muslims pay their *Zakat* during the month of *Ramadan.* This is because we get more reward from Allah ﷻ for every good deed we do in Ramadan. Let us remember to pay our share of *Zakat* when we grow older.

> ## WE HAVE LEARNED
> - *Zakat* is *Fard* on Muslims.
> - We should pay 2.5% of our wealth to poor and needy Muslims.
> - *Zakat* means to purify.

DO YOU KNOW THESE WORDS?
- *Zakat*
- *Fard*
- pure
- greed
- generous

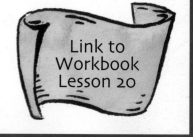

Link to
Workbook
Lesson 20

Aliya and Her Family Go to Makkah

TUNE IN:

- Something very special takes place in the month of *Dhu-al- Hijjah.*
Can you tell what is it?

Aliya and her parents are getting ready to go on a very special trip.

It is the fourth day of the month of *Dhu-al- Hijjah.*
They are leaving to go to Makkah for *Hajj.*

Hajj is the fifth pillar of Islam. Allah ﷻ asks every Muslim to go for *Hajj* at least once in his or her life. It is *Fard* upon every adult Muslim, except for the people who are too sick to travel, or people who do not have enough money to make the trip.

Aliya and her family take a plane from Vancouver in Canada to the city of Jeddah in Saudi Arabia. They stay at a hotel in Jeddah for one night.

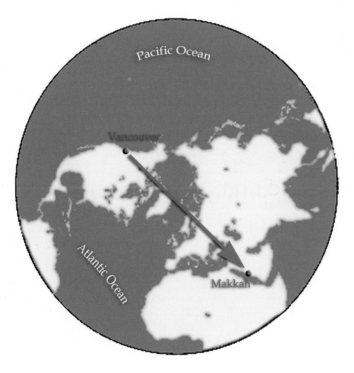

The next morning they take a shower and change into a special *Hajj* outfit. It is called *Ihram*. Aliya's father's *Ihram* is only two large white sheets and thick towels. He wraps them around his body.

Aliya and her mother ware long dresses with long sleeves. Their *Ihram* is a large scarf. They cover their heads with their *Ihram*.

Then they offer two *Raka'at Salah* and make the *Niyyah* (intention) for *Hajj.* Aliya and her parents leave for Makkah to visit the Ka'bah and perform *Hajj.*

It is a very special time in Makkah. Muslims from all over the world come here to perform *Hajj,* all at the same time. They all wear the same style *Ihram.* There is no difference between rich and poor, black and white or Arab and non-Arab.

There are thousands of people around! Aliya has to keep holding the hands of her father and mother. She does not want to get lost in the crowd.

They go to the Masjid al-Haram and make special *Du'as* as they looked at the Ka'bah.

They go around the Ka'bah seven times. This is called *Tawwaf.*

Then they offer two *Raka'at Salah*. Drink some *Zamzam* water and go to do *Sa'i*.

They walk between the hills of *Saffa* and *Marwa* seven times. This ends the *Sa'i*. At the end of the *Sa'i*, they make special *Du'as* with all the other *Hujjaj*.

After these *Du'as*, they clip their hair a little. It is late and they are tired. They go to their hotel room to take some rest.

> ## WE HAVE LEARNED
> - *Hajj* is the fifth pillar of Islam.
> - Men and women wear an *Ihram*.
> - *Hajj* is a very special time in Makkah.

DO YOU KNOW THESE WORDS?
- *Niyyah*
- *Ihram*
- *Dhu-al-Hijjah*
- *Tawwaf*
- *Sa'i*

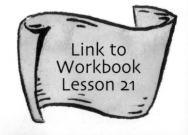

Link to Workbook Lesson 21

Tent city of Mina

On the eighth day of *Dhu-al-Hijjah,* Aliya's family leaves Makkah to go to Mina with other *Hujjaj.* Mina is a valley about three miles from Makkah.

Aliya sees thousands of tents set up in the valley of Mina. Her family stays in a comfortable tent.

Wadi of Arafat

On the ninth day of *Dhu-al-Hijjah,* Aliya and her parents go to the Valley of Arafat with other people in their group. They all stay in the Valley of Arafat for the whole day until *Maghrib* time. This is the main day of *Hajj.* Everyone spends all their time in praying to Allah ﷻ and reading the Qur'an.

Every one prays *Zuhr* and *Asr Salah* together in Arafat. It is a Sunnah because Rasulullah ﷺ did the same when he went for *Hajj.*

A night in Muzdalifah

Soon after sunset Aliya and her family left Arafat for Muzdalifah with all other *Hujjaj.* They all prayed Maghrib and 'Isha Salah together. They spend most of the night in Muzdalifah.

Return to Minah and stoning the *Shaitan*

Soon after Fajr prayers everyone leaves Muzdalifah for Mina.
There are three pillars in Mina,
each one represents *Shaitan*.
Hujjaj stone the biggest *Shaitan*
after they return to Mina.

Animal sacrifice

Aliya's father now goes to
sacrifice three goats. One for each person in the family.
Then they clip their hair and change into their normal clothes.
They do not need the *Ihram* anymore.

Aliya and her parents stay in Mina for two more days. They
go to stone the other two *Shaitan* as well, one on the 11th
and other on the 12th of *Dhu-al-Hijjah.*

Tawwaf az - Ziyarah

On the 11th of *Dhu-al-Hijjah* Aliya goes back to Makkah with
her parents to make *Tawwaf* of the *Ka'bah*.
This is called *Tawwaf az-Ziyarah.*

The family leaves Mina on the 12th of *Dhu-al-Hijjah* and comes to Makkah. They are
very tired. They stay in a comfortable hotel
in Makkah for one day.

A visit to Madinah, the City of the Prophet ﷺ

The next day Aliya and her parents leave Makkah for Madinah. Madinah is the city of Prophet Muhammad ﷺ. They go to Madinah to give *Salam* to the Prophet ﷺ and visit the *Masjid an-Nabi.* Aliya loves the city of Madinah.

WE HAVE LEARNED

- All *Hujjaj* go to the tent city of Mina to stay on the 8th of *Dhu-al-Hijjah.*
- The ninth of *Dhu-al-Hijjah* is the main day of *Hajj*
- Everyone, who goes to *Hajj* spends the ninth of *Dhu-al-Hijjah* in the valley of Arafat.
- The *Hujjaj* go to *Muzdalifah* right after sunset from Mina and spend the night there.
- They returned to Mina on the 10th of *Dhu-al-Hijjah* and stone the Big *Shaitan.*
- On the 10th they get their hair cut, make the sacrifice and change into normal clothes.
- Everyone makes the last *Tawwaf* of the Ka'bah on the 11th of *Dhu-al-Hijjah.* This is called *Tawwaf az-Ziyarah.*

DO YOU KNOW THESE WORDS?
- Mina
- Arafat
- Muzdalifah
- *Tawwaf az-Ziyarah*
- comfortable
- valley

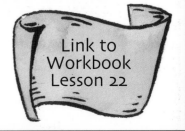

Link to Workbook Lesson 22

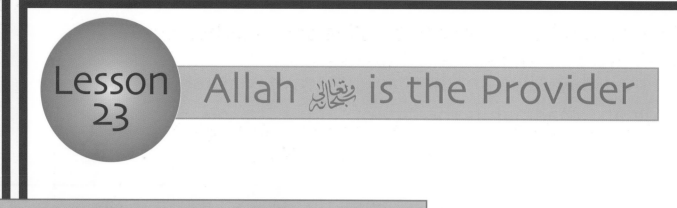

Lesson 23 — Allah ﷻ is the Provider

TUNE IN:

• Allah ﷻ says in the Qur'an:

إِنَّ ٱللَّهَ هُوَ ٱلرَّزَّاقُ ذُو ٱلْقُوَّةِ ٱلْمَتِينُ

"Indeed, Allah is the Provider, the Lord of Power, the Strong" (*Al-Zariyat*:58)

Allah ﷻ is the Provider, *Ar-Razzaq*. He provides us with all the things we need. He gives us the food and the drinks that we eat and drink every day. He gives us the clothes we wear. The homes we live in and the money we have is all from Allah ﷻ.

إِنَّ ٱللَّهَ هُوَ ٱلرَّزَّاقُ ذُو ٱلْقُوَّةِ ٱلْمَتِينُ

"Indeed, Allah is the Provider,
the Lord of Power, Strong."
(*Al-Zariyat*: 58)

Allah ﷻ provides us with everything we need to live in this world. Food and water are gifts of Allah ﷻ.

We need food and water to be alive and healthy. We need fresh, clean air and bright sunlight to live.

The plants and animals also need food, water, air and sunlight to live. We get our food from plants and animals.

Allah ﷻ is the only One, who provides us with food, water, air and sunlight to live. He says in the Qur'an:

قُلْ مَن يَرْزُقُكُم مِّنَ ٱلسَّمَـٰوَٰتِ وَٱلْأَرْضِ ۖ قُلِ ٱللَّهُ ۖ

"Say: Who gives you sustenance, from the heavens and the earth? Say: ' it is Allah...''
(*Saba*: 24)

Allah ﷻ is the Provider of everything, but He wants us to look for only *Halal* food. Allah ﷻ tells us in the Qur'an:

يَـٰٓأَيُّهَا ٱلنَّاسُ كُلُوا۟ مِمَّا فِى ٱلۡأَرۡضِ حَلَـٰلًا طَيِّبًا

"O mankind! Eat out of that which is on earth,
Halal and good". (*Al-Baqarah*: 168)

Alhamdulillah! Allah ﷻ is our Provider. He is *Al-Razzaq*. We are thankful to Allah ﷻ for giving us life and providing us with the things that we need to live.

WE HAVE LEARNED

- Allah ﷻ is *Ar-Razzaq*. He is the Provider of all the things His creations need.
- We need water, food, sunlight, and air to live on this earth.
- We should be thankful to Allah ﷻ for giving us all the things we need.

DO YOU KNOW THESE WORDS?
- *Ar-Razzaq*
- sunlight
- Provider
- earth
- Bright

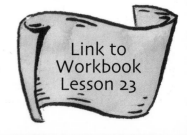
Link to
Workbook
Lesson 23

EATING *HALAL* FOOD

Allah  tells us in the Qur'an:

يَـٰٓأَيُّهَا ٱلنَّاسُ كُلُواْ مِمَّا فِى ٱلْأَرْضِ حَلَـٰلًا طَيِّبًا

"O Mankind! Eat out of that which is on earth,
Halal and good."(Al-Baqarah: 168)

Read the *Ayah* above and think of the things we need that Allah ﷻ has provided for us to live a healthy life. Write your answers in the diagram using the points given.

CAUSE   EFFECT

Three important things we need
to live:

Type of food we can eat:

We live and grow
to be healthy and
strong Muslims

Other things we can take to
make us strong and healthy:

What does Allah ﷻ Tell Us about Food?

TUNE IN:

- Food helps us to grow. We need to eat food to be strong and healthy. However some kinds of food can make us sick and hurt our bodies and minds.

اَلْعَلِيمُ

Allah ﷻ is *Al-'Alim*, He knows what is good and what is bad for us.   Allah ﷻ wants us to be safe. He also wants us to have a pure heart, a pure mind and a pure body.

Food is one of the most important things we need to live. Allah ﷻ wants us to eat food that is good and healthy.

We eat food to make our bodies healthy and strong. When we are strong and healthy, we can do a lot of 'Ibadah to Allah ﷻ. Eating and drinking is a form of 'Ibadah too.

Allah ﷻ likes us to be healthy and pure in our hearts, minds and bodies. In order to be pure we need to eat the food that is permitted by Allah ﷻ and be thankful to Him. Allah ﷻ says in the Qur'an:

كُلُواْ مِن رِّزْقِ رَبِّكُمْ وَٱشْكُرُواْ لَهُ

" Eat of the food provided by your Lord, and be grateful to Him " (*Saba:* 15)

We should eat the food which Allah ﷻ tells us to eat. This food is *Halal* for us.

We do not eat food which Allah ﷻ forbids us to eat. This food is *Haram* for us. We shall learn more about *Halal* and *Haram* foods in the next lesson.

WE HAVE LEARNED

- Allah ﷻ permits us to eat good food that is called *Halal* food.
- Allah ﷻ forbids us from eating foods that are not good for us. These are called *Haram* foods.
- We eat healthy foods to be strong.

DO YOU KNOW THESE WORDS?

- Healthy
- *Ibadah*
- strong
- permitted

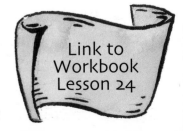

Link to Workbook Lesson 24

Lesson 25 — *Halal* Food and Drinks

TUNE IN:

- Food and drink is important for our health. The food we take must be both healthy and *Halal*

Food and drinks are important for our health. Islam gives us rules about how Muslims should take their food and drink. This is important for both our minds and our bodies.

Allah ﷻ allows all good and pure things to be used for food and drink. The Qur'an says:

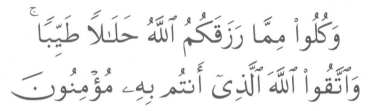

"Eat of the things which Allah has provided for you,
lawful and good, but be conscious of Allah, in whom you believe"
(Al-Ma'idah: 88)

Halal and *Haram* are Arabic words. *Halal* means "allowed" and *Haram* means "not allowed". *Halal* things are lawful. *Haram* things are unlawful. Allah ﷻ made most foods and drinks *Halal* for us.

Let us find out some of the foods which Allah ﷻ made *Halal* for Muslims.

All fish and vegetables are *Halal* foods.

The meat of some animals is also *Halal* for Muslims.

SOME ANIMALS WHOSE MEAT IS *HALAL*

SOME BIRDS WHOSE MEAT IS *HALAL*

Sometimes we buy food from shops and supermarkets. We should read the labels carefully to make sure that they only have *Halal* ingredients.

Allah ﷻ wants us to use only *Halal* food and drinks. He wants us to have healthy bodies and a healthy minds. Eating *Halal* food is obligatory upon every Muslim.

WE HAVE LEARNED

- Eating *Halal* food is obligatory upon every Muslim.
- Fish and vegetables are examples of *Halal* food.
- The meat of some animals is *Halal* for Muslims.

DO YOU KNOW THESE WORDS?
- Lawful
- *Halal*
- *Haram*
- obligatory

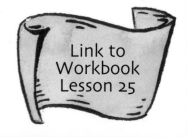

Link to Workbook Lesson 25

TUNE IN:

• Allah ﷻ forbids us in the Qur'an from eating some kinds of food.

"He has forbidden you dead meat, and blood , and the meat of a pig, and that on which any other name has been invoked besides that of Allah."
(Al- Baqarah: 173)

Let us find out about the food that is forbidden for us to eat.

Allah ﷻ forbids us from eating certain foods and using some drinks. These are called *Haram* food and drinks. We should not eat or drink things which are not allowed by Allah ﷻ.

Haram means "prohibited" or "unlawful". Allah ﷻ does not allow Muslims to eat or drink *Haram* food and drinks. Allah ﷻ tells us what is forbidden in the following *Ayah*:

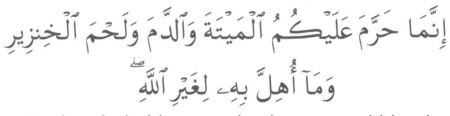

إِنَّمَا حَرَّمَ عَلَيْكُمُ ٱلْمَيْتَةَ وَٱلدَّمَ وَلَحْمَ ٱلْخِنزِيرِ
وَمَآ أُهِلَّ بِهِۦ لِغَيْرِ ٱللَّهِ

"He has forbidden you dead meat, and blood ,
and the meat of a pig, and that on which any other
name has been invoked besides that of Allah."
(*Al- Baqarah*: 173)

In this *Ayah*, Allah ﷻ tells us the foods that are forbidden for us. These foods are called *Haram*:

1. The meat of dead animals.
2. The blood of any animal.
3. The flesh of pigs (pork, ham or lard)
4. The meat of animals which are not slaughtered in Allah's name.

All kinds of alcoholic drinks, such as beer and wine, are *Haram*. They are harmful to the body and mind. Rasulullah ﷺ said in a *Hadith*:

"Every drink that intoxicates is *Haram*"
(Sahih Muslim)

We must only eat foods and drinks that Allah ﷻ has permitted us to use. We should follow the rules as best as we can so that we can be healthy, bright, and blessed.

SOME ANIMALS WHOSE MEAT IS *HARAM*

SOME BIRDS WHOSE MEAT IS *HARAM*

WE HAVE LEARNED

- Food and drinks that are forbidden by Allah ﷻ are *Haram* for us.
- The meat of dead animals, meat of pigs and the meat of animals not slaughtered in Allah's name are *Haram* for us.
- We should not eat food items that are *Haram* because they are not good for us.

DO YOU KNOW THESE WORDS?
- alcoholic
- forbidden
- unlawful
- harmful

Link to Workbook Lesson 26

Lesson 27 — Respect for Parents

TUNE IN:

- The Prophet ﷺ said, "Best among us are those who are kind to their parents"

After obedience to Allah ﷻ and His Messenger, obedience to one's parents is most important. The Qur'an asks us to be respectful and polite to our parents:

وَقَضَىٰ رَبُّكَ أَلَّا تَعْبُدُوٓا۟ إِلَّآ إِيَّاهُ وَبِٱلْوَٰلِدَيْنِ إِحْسَٰنًا

إِمَّا يَبْلُغَنَّ عِندَكَ ٱلْكِبَرَ أَحَدُهُمَآ أَوْ كِلَاهُمَا

فَلَا تَقُل لَّهُمَآ أُفٍّ وَلَا تَنْهَرْهُمَا وَقُل لَّهُمَا قَوْلًا كَرِيمًا ۝

وَٱخْفِضْ لَهُمَا جَنَاحَ ٱلذُّلِّ مِنَ ٱلرَّحْمَةِ وَقُل

رَّبِّ ٱرْحَمْهُمَا كَمَا رَبَّيَانِى صَغِيرًا ۝

"Your Lord commands that you worship none but Him, and that you be kind to parents. Whether one or both of them reach old age in your life, say not to them a word of anger, nor repel but address them in terms of honor, and out of kindness, lower to them your wing of humility, and say: My Lord ! bestow on them Your Mercy, even as they cherished me in childhood."

(Surah Al-Isra 17:23-4)

Our parents work very hard to take good care of us. They help us when we are little. They get us all the things we need. Some times they even spend a lot of their money to buy things we want.

When we are sick they stay awake all night and take care of us. When we are sad, they feel sad. When we are happy, they are happy. They are kind and loving to our friends.

Parents teach us how to read and write. They help us with our homework. They teach us good manners, and help us grow to be nice people. Best of all, they help us to read the Qur'an.

Let us pray to Allah ﷻ to keep our parents healthy and safe. Let us try to do everything we can to make our parents happy. Let us work hard to make them proud of us. Let us listen to what they say to us. Let us do as they tell us to do.

Let us help our parents with the chores around the house. We can help them by cleaning the house, washing clothes, mowing the lawn etc. When we help them they know that we love and respect them.

Let us make sure that we are always there when they need us. As they become older and weak, we should be as patient with our older parents as they were to us when we were little. Let us make special *Du'a* for our parents.

WE HAVE LEARNED

- Muslims should be obedient to their parents.
- We must be polite and loving to our mother and father.
- We should take special care of our parents when they get old.

DO YOU KNOW THESE WORDS?

- Obedience
- disobey
- advice
- special

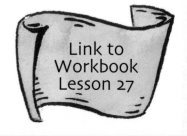

Link to Workbook Lesson 27

TUNE IN:

• Respect for the elders and kindness to the younger are the qualities of a Muslim.

Haniya and Jibraan are good Muslim children. They are loving and kind to those who are younger than them. They also show respect for their elders. Haniya and Jibraan are respectful, polite and kind to their elders. Their elders are happy with them. They treat them kindly and always remember them in their *Du'a*.

Rasulullah ﷺ told us :

$$لَيْسَ مِنَّا مَنْ لَمْ يَرْحَمْ صَغِيرَنَا ، وَيُوَقِّرْ كَبِيرَنَا$$

"He who does not show respect to those older and does not
show kindness to those younger is not from us"
(Al – Tirmidhi)

Haniya and Jibraan respect their parents and grandparents. They also respect their uncles and aunts. Let us all be like Haniya and Jibraan and talk to our elders with respect and kindness.

Miss Marshall is Haniya's teacher. She is always respectful to Miss Marshall. Miss Marshall helps Haniya learn many things. She teaches her how to read and write. We all should respect our teachers. It is our duty to love and obey our teachers.

Akbar is Haniya's friend and neighbor. His house is next to Haniya's house. He lives with his parents and little sister. His grandparents live with him. When Haniya goes to Akbar's house, she always says *As-Salamu 'Alaikum* to Akbar's parents and grandparents. She also helps AKbar's mother if she needs any help. Let us try to be like Haniya and respect our neighbors.

WE HAVE LEARNED
- We should respect our elders.
- We should listen to our teachers.
- We should help our neighbors

DO YOU KNOW THESE WORDS?
- elders
- respectful
- polite
- neighbors

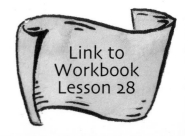

Link to Workbook Lesson 28

TUNE IN:
- A *Masjid* is the House of Allah ﷻ. Those who build and maintain a *Masjid* love Allah ﷻ.

A *Masjid* is a place where we worship Allah ﷻ alone. He is happy with us when we help build a *Masjid* and keep it clean. He also wants us to pray in the *Masjid*. The Qur'an teaches us:

إِنَّمَا يَعْمُرُ مَسَاجِدَ ٱللَّهِ مَنْ ءَامَنَ بِٱللَّهِ
وَٱلْيَوْمِ ٱلْأَخِرِ وَأَقَامَ ٱلصَّلَوٰةَ وَءَاتَى ٱلزَّكَوٰةَ وَلَمْ يَخْشَ إِلَّا ٱللَّهَ

"Indeed, he shall build and maintain a *Masjid* of Allah,
who believes in Allah, and the Last Day, offers regular prayer,
and gives the *Zakah* and fears none except Allah."

(At-Tawbah 9:18)

ADAB OF VISITING A MASJID

It is a *Sunnah* to enter the *Masjid* with the right foot in first and say this *Du'a*: اَللَّهُمَّ افْتَحْ لِي أَبْوَابَ رَحْمَتِك

"O Allah! Open the doors of Your *Rahmah* for me"

It is important to take off our shoes when we enter the prayer area. We do not want to bring any dirt from the street into the prayer hall.

We should keep the prayer rug of the *Masjid* specially clean as people offer their prayers there. They also do *Sajdah* to Allah ﷻ.

We need to do *Wudu* before entering the *Masjid*. We should always try to get to the *Masjid* before the *Iqamah* is called.

It is a *Sunnah* to perform two *Raka'at* of *Salah* silently as we enter the *Masjid*. This prayer is called *Tahiyyat al-Masjid*.

We sit down quietly in the prayer hall and wait for the *Salah* to begin. We should not talk or play games in the prayer hall. It is better to read the Qur'an and think of Allah ﷻ.

When the *Iqamah* is called, all of us should stand in straight rows behind the *Imam*. Every one stands close to each other, leaving no gaps in between. We should make straight rows.

The women stand behind men or in their own special areas in the *Masjid*.

We may stay in the *Masjid* for *Sunnah* and *Nafl* prayers. It is a *Sunnah* to leave the *Masjid* with the left foot first. We say this *Du'a*:

$$اَللَّهُمَّ إِنِّي أَسْأَلُكَ مِنْ فَضْلِكَ.$$

"O Allah! I ask you to bless me with Your *Fadl* (Generosity)."

Prophet Muhammad ﷺ has said that the reward of offering *Salah* with *Jama'ah* is 27 times more than offering it alone. Let us make special effort to go to the *Masjid* for all our prayers.

WE HAVE LEARNED
- The *Masjid* is the House of Allah ﷻ.
- We should try to offer our *Salah* with *Jama'ah* in the *Masjid*.
- We must take our shoes off and do *Wudu* before we enter the prayer hall of the *Masjid*.

DO YOU KNOW THESE WORDS?
- Worship
- *Nafl*
- *Sajdah*
- punctuality
- *Iqamah*
- regularity

Link to Workbook Lesson 29

Lesson 30 — Etiquettes of *Salah*

Etiquettes of *Salah*

TUNE IN:

- Ali has to go to a football game. He prays in a hurry, thinking about the game. How should we offer our *Salah*?

Salah is the most important part of our faith. Rasulullah ﷺ has taught us that *Salah* is a very special blessing of Allah ﷻ. We should offer it with great care and love for Allah ﷻ.

TAHARA

It is important that we are clean and pure when we stand up in front of Allah ﷻ for *Salah*. We should perform proper *Wudu*. We should wear pure and clean clothes and cover ourselves well. Prophet ﷺ said:

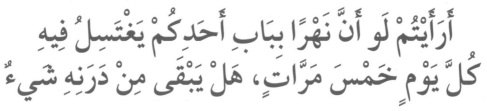

أَرَأَيْتُمْ لَوْ أَنَّ نَهْرًا بِبَابِ أَحَدِكُمْ يَغْتَسِلُ فِيهِ كُلَّ يَوْمٍ خَمْسَ مَرَّاتٍ، هَلْ يَبْقَى مِنْ دَرَنِهِ شَيْءٌ

"Salah is like washing in a river outside our door five times a day. Salah washes our sins".

PUNCTUALITY

When the time for *Salah* comes, we should leave everything we are doing and stand up for *Salah*. It is important to offer each *Salah* on time without any delay.

REGULARITY

When we do something again and again it becomes a habit. We feel uncomfortable if we do not do it. It is the same way when we offer *Salah* five times every day. It becomes our habit. We feel uncomfortable if we miss offering the *Salah*. Let us develop a habit of praying every day, five times on time.

NOT IN A HURRY

We should be relaxed when we pray. We should not hurry, wiggle, or throw our bodies around when we are praying. It is important that we take our time to complete the *Salah* and remain calm.

WE HAVE LEARNED
- *Salah* is our duty towards Allah ﷻ.
- We should be punctual and regular in offering *Salah*.
- It is important to be relaxed when offering the *Salah*.

DO YOU KNOW THESE WORDS?
- Relaxed
- calm
- important
- punctuality

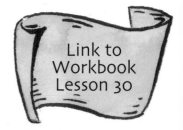

Link to Workbook Lesson 30

Lesson 31 — Kind Words and Actions

TUNE IN:

وَأَحْسِن كَمَا أَحْسَنَ ٱللَّهُ إِلَيْكَ

"Be kind, as Allah has been kind to you".
(Al-Qasas 28:77)

Allah ﷻ is Most Kind and Most Merciful. He made us because He is Kind. He gave us our families. He takes care of us. We cannot count all the gifts that Allah ﷻ has given us.

We must thank Him for His Kindness. The best way to thank Allah ﷻ is to be kind to others. This means that we speak to everyone in a nice way. We should also help those who need help.

We should not hurt anyone with our words or our actions. It is important to respect everyone's right. When we do any favour to someone we should not expect anything in return from him or her. Instead we should think of the many more favors Allah ﷻ has given us.

وَقُل لِّعِبَادِى يَقُولُوا ٱلَّتِى هِىَ أَحْسَنُ

"And say to My servants that they should only say those things that are best…"
(al-Isra': 53)

The reward of a Muslim is with Allah ﷻ. His Kindness and Mercy is the best reward we could have. Rasulullah ﷺ said:

$$\text{خَيْرُ النَّاسِ أَنْفَعُهُمْ لِلنَّاسِ}$$

"The best person is one who benefits other people"

(Minawi)

The Qur'an and the *Sunnah* of our Prophet ﷺ teach us how to be kind and helpful to others. Allah ﷻ is Merciful. Our Prophet Muhammad ﷺ was sent as the Mercy to the worlds. We must be kind and merciful to all human beings. We should be kind to animals and all the things created by Allah ﷻ.

WE HAVE LEARNED

- A Muslim must always speak politely and be kind to all human beings.
- The best way to thank Allah ﷻ is to be kind and helpful to others.
- We should be kind to all animals.

DO YOU KNOW THESE WORDS?
- blessings
- gratitude
- kindness
- respect

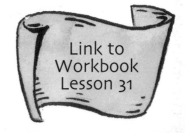

Link to Workbook Lesson 31